The Survival Toolbox

67 Practical Tools and Supplies to Fix or Maintain Your Home After Disaster Strikes

by Damian Brindle

===> Get dozens of free survival guides, hundreds of videos, 600+ "how to" articles, gear reviews and so much more here: https://rethinksurvival.com

Disclaimer

The material covered within is for informational purposes only. I take no responsibility for what you do with this knowledge and I cannot be held responsible for any property or medical damages caused by the items or information you read about within. I would advise you to check your local laws as it's possible that some of the items or advice I offer may be illegal in some areas, and I would highly advise you against their use in said areas. Moreover, by using any information or material found within, you assume all risks for the material covered. You agree to indemnify, hold harmless, and defend the author, Damian Brindle, from all claims and damages arising from the use, possession or consequences of the information covered. By taking and/or using any informational resources found within, you agree that you will use this information in a safe and legal manner, consistent with all applicable laws, safety rules, and good common sense. You further agree that you will take such steps as may be reasonably necessary or required by applicable law to keep any information out of the hands of minors as well as untrained and/or irresponsible individuals.

Table of Contents

Introduction (Notes to Readers, Plus Free Stuff)

This book is intended to provide you with a comprehensive list of hand tools that may be useful after a disaster with the expectation that you'll know how to use them. As such, it's written to be fast to read and includes minimal product images. Links are provided to specific products should you want additional information or to purchase the product.

About Website Links

Realize, too, that this was originally written to be an electronic book only with many website links referenced throughout. Because this is a paperback book, however, referencing these links can be tedious if you had to type them into your web browser by hand. To make this easier on you, I have consolidated all referenced links into one page here: https://rethinksurvival.com/books/toolbox-links.html.

When new links are introduced they will be referenced with superscripts which will then correspond to the appropriate URL on the above referenced website page.

For completeness, however, all referenced links will also be included in Appendix B.

Grab Your Free 67-Point Checklist

Odds are that you won't remember everything listed when you're done reading this book. To make your life easier I've created a free, easy-to-reference 67-point toolbox checklist which you can download that outlines all the tools and supplies discussed herein. You'll find a link to it here (so that you can follow along if you like) as well as at the end of this book, but please do read the entire book first.

Now, download your free, easy-to-reference 67-point toolbox checklist here.[1]

Prepare Yourself for Natural Disaster in Only 5 Minutes

Since you clearly understand the need for safety, I want to share with you my unique **5 Minute Survival Blueprint** where you'll discover just how to keep your family safe and secure from disasters of all kinds in only 5 minutes a day, fast, easy, and inexpensively.[2]

More Survival Books You'll Enjoy

If you liked what you read when finished, you can find more survival books I've written at https://rethinksurvival.com/kindle-books/.[3]

This Book's Tone

As noted before, this book is written in a quick, simple, easy to read format. Hence, it is presented in a "Conversational" form and not one that is intended to be grammatically correct. Getting YOU and your family ready for emergencies is the sole focus of this book.

And My Thanks...

I also want to thank those folks who took the time to review this book, to offer their own suggestions, and to correct my mistakes... you know who you are.

Why Would I Need a Survival Toolbox?

Having the gear and supplies to see you through the aftermath of a disaster is crucial to a successful recovery effort. Most people take this to mean having useful gear like water filters and flashlights as well as any number of supplies, including food, batteries, and fuel.

While these items are all great to have on hand—and I certainly have them myself—a quality set of hand tools should be considered nearly as important as water filters and flashlights because of what they allow you to accomplish should the need arise. After all, have you ever tried to drive a nail without a hammer, or turn a bolt without a wrench? Odds are you haven't, and you wouldn't even consider trying to do so because it's just too difficult without the right tool for the job. Tools make otherwise simple tasks like these possible.

Recovering after a disaster, however, may not be so simple. In fact, there could be a lot of work to do! For example, you could find that windows have been broken, your roof has a hole in it, or a wall has been severely damaged. Damage to your home such as this could make your survival that much more difficult and maybe even dangerous, in some cases. Having the proper tools to fix and maintain your primary dwelling helps to ensure you stay safe.

Of course, I cannot guarantee that you'll need to use any of these tools whatsoever. It could be that your home remains unscathed during a disaster, which would be ideal. But the entire point in prepping is to always plan for the worst and hope for the best, and a handy toolbox such as this one helps you do precisely that.

Besides, this very same toolbox can be quickly added to your vehicle during a bug out, given to a friend or neighbor in need, or act as a backup set of supplies should your primary set of tools be compromised during a disaster.

What If You've Never Even Used a Hammer Before?

If you've never wielded a hammer before or even turned a wrench, that's ok. It could be that somebody you know—such as a neighbor—does know their way around a hammer, wrench, or saw and could make use of the equipment to help you out. In any case, tools cannot be useful to anyone if you don't have them in the first place.

Look at it this way: the idea is like having a set of jumper cables in your car even if you don't know how to use them yourself; somebody is bound to come along who does know how to use them and who can, therefore, help you jumpstart your car and get on the road again.

That said, I wouldn't always bet on a friendly neighbor stopping by to help. If you have no idea how to use any of the tools discussed within then I would encourage you to do some additional research into how and maybe even find somebody is willing to show you.

Where Can I Find the Tools I Need?

Your local hardware store or even many Walmart stores will certainly sell most of the hand tools I discuss within. That said, I wouldn't buy most of these tools new. Instead, look for used tools at local garage sales, thrift stores, or even ask friends and family if they have anything extra. Odds are that you know somebody who has an enormous number of tools, so much so that they may be willing to part with a few of them to get you started.

Personally, I've accumulated tools from many sources over the years, including hand-me-downs, garage sales, Goodwill stores, and more. Once upon a time I even received a vehicle toolkit which included some basics when we signed up with our local bank years ago. The toolkit wasn't the best set of tools whatsoever, but it was free and better than nothing.

What About Power Tools?

This list focuses solely on hand tools for your recovery efforts. The reason being is because you cannot expect to rely on grid power immediately after disaster. Hand tools, on the other hand, are always useful and functional no matter what happens to the power grid.

Of course, if you can supply power to your power tools—either because the grid is functioning, or you have an off-grid power source—then you should surely make use of them to speed up your recover efforts.

How Much Will This Cost?

Cost will largely depend on how you acquire your tools. If you buy them brand new at a retail store then I could see you spending a few hundred dollars at least, possibly several hundred if you buy quality tools. On the contrary, a garage sale could cost you well less than $100 dollars if you're lucky enough to find what you may be missing, but this will take some time. Tools from friends or family may even be free.

Personally, I put my survival toolbox together with extra tools which I had lying around, so, besides the cost of a better toolbox that I recently bought for this very purpose, the cost to me was minimal. Remember, too, that this doesn't have to be completed in a day; take some time to piece this together and you'll probably save even more money.

Where Should I Keep My Survival Toolbox?

I happen to have a detached garage where I live. I keep all my primary tools out there, everything from power tools and hand tools to yard equipment and even some food storage. If, heaven-forbid, a tree ever fell on my garage then I may find that most of my tools have been damaged or simply inaccessible as a result. Clearly, if the tools in my detached garage were the only ones I had to rely upon then I could be in trouble should I even needed them for my family's survival.

That's where a simple toolbox like this comes in. I fill it with the hand tools and supplies that I think I might need to repair my home and then I keep it stored away from my primary set of tools. In my case that's my actual house, specifically in a basement closet. If this set of tools also becomes compromised during the same disaster, then odds are that I have a much bigger problem than even this set of tools can help me deal with. In this case I should bug out!

Another option would have been to keep the toolbox in my vehicle (assuming I don't park in the garage, which I don't) but I already have plenty of other survival items—as well as some basic hand tools—inside my car and, so, this toolbox would simply take up too much additional space. As such, the basement closet is where this backup survival toolbox ended up.

What works for your situation? I don't know. Just do your best to NOT keep this toolbox anywhere near your primary set of tools so that you have a backup set to rely upon.

What Toolbox to Choose?

There are many toolbox choices out there. You don't need anything fancy whatsoever, though, a larger toolbox will obviously fit more supplies. That said, even a basic $20 or less toolbox should work just fine. As an example, for years I used a Stanley toolbox for this very purpose:

But it was bulging with stuff and didn't even fit everything that I wanted to include. Recently, I upgraded to a Ridgid toolbox which was a bit bigger and is clearly sturdier:

Fortunately, there are plenty of other toolbox options to choose from, everything from a soft-sided tool bag to a mobile toolbox that has wheels and a convenient pull handle. There are nesting toolboxes, metal ones, toolboxes with assorted organizers included, and more. You're sure to find one that fits your needs and budget.

The mobile toolbox may, in fact, be the perfect solution for those with mobility issues or if you expect to have a lot of ground to cover around your home. I thought most mobile toolboxes were a bit too big for where I wanted to store it, otherwise I probably would have chosen one.

No matter what you choose to use, the toolbox will be heavy. For instance, my toolbox filled with tools weighs right at fifty pounds. That's a heavy load to carry any distance at all. Honestly, I tried to pare it down, but still ended up with a heavier toolbox than I would have preferred. Unfortunately, it's hard to get around the weight issue if you want a toolset that's truly useful for when you need it most.

With that in mind, let's get onto the tools...

The List of Tools

Please be aware that the following list of tools are in no particular order for survival purposes. They are, nevertheless, generally photographed to group similar items together. Near the end the item groupings get a bit haphazard, I must admit, but that's because I attempted to photograph as many of the smaller items in one shot as I could.

Note, too, that there are a handful of items which probably aren't very necessary in a survival toolkit such as this. Items like the nail punch and mini level that I mention later come to mind. They were included here simply because they were very small, lightweight, and I had extras. Most everything else, on the other hand, could prove to be very useful to you in your time of need; I would encourage you to include as much as you can in your toolbox.

Safety Gear (dust masks, eyeglasses, ear plugs, and gloves)

I'm a firm believer in being safe. It's why I tell my kids to wear their seatbelts in the car, why I tell my youngest to wear a helmet while riding his scooter, and why I wear ear muffs when using lawn equipment.

Sometimes you know that an activity may be potentially dangerous, such as when using a chainsaw, but most times you just never know if or when something might happen. And because accidents tend to happen so fast that you won't have time to react, you need to be proactive, and that's why we'll start with safety gear first.

Here's a few thoughts...

1. Dust Masks, several (preferably N-95 rated)

Even the most basic dust mask will help to minimize direct contact of airborne substances with your mouth and nose, but they won't do much more than that. For that you need a better mask, such as an N-95 mask that most preppers stockpile. Even so, N-95 rated masks aren't perfect either, though, they are a better choice than a basic dust mask for most situations.

I would, at the very least, encourage you to purchase N-95 masks with a one-way exhalation valve which makes them far more comfortable to wear for longer periods of time; they're a bit more expensive, but well worth the investment.[4]

Note: If you're unaware, masks are made for different purposes and have different efficiency ratings. This article on How to Choose a Respirator or Dust Mask explains the differences well.[5]

2. Safety Glasses

Protecting your eyes from any sort of impact is crucial, especially when you're working in or around your home after a disaster. And if you're going to be hammering or sawing or prying on things—and you probably will be if you've got this toolbox out—then eye protection is a must.

Even times when you don't think anything can happen you should wear them. For example, a while back I was helping my son glue the end of a pair of headphones and when I snapped the pieces together a bit of superglue shot back at my face, very near my eye. I thought it hit me in the eye for a moment; it did not. Regrettably, I wasn't wearing safety glasses at the time, but that experience reminded me why I should always choose to wear safety gear if I'm doing anything out of the ordinary.

Ensure the safety glasses you get are "ANSI-compliant" or "impact rated," usually indicated by a "Z87+" marking somewhere. For even better protection, consider military-grade ballistic eyewear or "shooters" glasses.[6] These glasses are usually held to a higher standard than those rated for civilian use. You can learn more about ballistic-rated eyewear here.[7]

3. Ear Protection (e.g., ear plugs)

Even if you won't be using loud power tools or yard equipment after a disaster—the most common reasons for using hearing protection these days—you could still be exposed to other loud noises, such as a running generator, loud banging from hammering, or near somebody using a chainsaw to cut up a fallen tree, for example. Consider including more than one set so others have a pair available or in case you lose them, which is easy to do.

Alternatively, choose a pair of quality ear muffs for even better hearing protection, many of which fold up to a relatively small profile. And, similar to eye protection, there are better options available. No matter whether you choose ear plugs or ear muffs, a higher decibel (dB) rating means better protection with between 22-34 dB as the expected noise reduction range.[8]

4. Leather Gloves, fitted

Get a pair of leather-palmed, form-fitting work gloves which fit you and maybe one more pair for another person with the expectation that you'll have some help after a disaster. Don't skimp on quality gloves for the simple fact they're so useful in many situations, even those you may not have thought of.

For example, even just trying to hold onto a tool that's cold or wet for any length of time make a pair of gloves a welcome addition. And that's to say nothing for grabbing debris that may be sharp or otherwise dangerous to you, or simply hard to handle with your bare hands alone. Gloves also help protect your hands from direct infections and even contact with potentially infectious materials.

5. Larger Work Gloves (bonus if fitted gloves can also fit inside)

Another set of gloves, especially a larger set than the ones that fit you, may also prove useful in case you need to offer a pair to someone else. Personally, I've found that I can fit a smaller pair of gloves inside this larger pair to offer additional protection for myself. If you're a large man with large hands then this won't be the case. At the very least, this larger set can used by almost anyone regardless of hand size.

6. Chemical Gloves, heavy-duty preferred

There are many types of protective gloves out there, each of which offer varying levels of protection depending on the pathogen. This Glove Selection Guide offers a good overview of how to select a pair of gloves as well as what gloves are best suited for what purpose.[9]

The pair I included here don't offer much protection and, therefore, should be considered "light duty" chemical gloves. Instead, try to get a pair or two of heavy-duty PVC-coated chemical gloves that, if possible, extend to your elbows for better protection.[10] Neoprene gloves may be an even better choice than PVC-coated if you can find them at a decent price.

BONUS: Hard Hat

A hard hat wasn't included in this toolkit list simply because it wouldn't fit inside. That said, a hard hat could be among the most important items to include in your safety gear because of the very real potential for something to come crashing down on your head after a disaster, from debris to broken tree limbs. Therefore, if you can include a hard hat in survival gear then that would be best.

Cutting Tools

Have you ever tried to cut something without a saw? Perhaps you have with a hatchet or axe but cutting lumber down to size or a piece of metal pipe to length isn't going to happen without an appropriate saw blade.

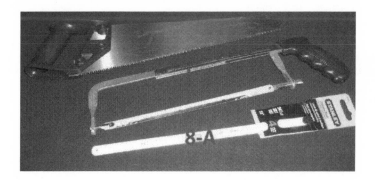

7. Crosscut Hand Saw, 15"

Although I'd prefer a longer hand saw (such as the Stanley 20-inch SharpTooth) to make cutting tasks faster, a small hand saw like this one will work just fine and fits nicely inside most any toolbox.[11] In fact, most any crosscut hand saw will last for a long time if it's well taken care of.

If you think you may do a lot of sawing post-disaster, then consider adding a second handsaw to your toolkit since they're inexpensive. You could also learn how to sharpen the teeth properly; you'll need a triangular file (not included in this kit) to do so... and a lot of patience.[12]

8. Hacksaw (with extra blades)

Whereas a crosscut hand saw is great for cutting lumber, they're useless for anything metal. A trusty hacksaw—with their very small and closely-spaced teeth—is great for cutting metal as well as some plastics. The blades can dull quickly, however, so be sure to have replacements.

Hammer, Wrecking Bar, Bolt Cutter

There's nothing like NOT having a hammer when you need one; there really is no good substitute. The wrecking bar and bolt cutters are also invaluable when needed as well, though, likely not as useful as the hammer.

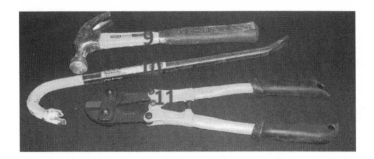

9. Claw Hammer, 16 oz.

If you've ever walked through the tool aisle of your local hardware store you're sure to notice the vast array of hammers available, everything from ball-peen and framing hammers to sledgehammers and mallets. Each hammer style has a specific use but, for our purposes, a general-purpose claw-style hammer is perfect.

I would've liked to include a small sledge hammer in your toolkit as well. And, while they're not very heavy (at about three or four pounds) they take up more space than I was comfortable with giving and did add extra weight.

A larger sledge hammer (of, say, eight to ten pounds) would be more useful after a disaster, in my opinion, because they can be used for demolition, driving stakes, and splitting wood (in conjunction with a log splitting wedge), to name a few uses. I would encourage you to have a larger one even though it won't fit in your toolbox.

10. Wrecking Bar, 18"

There are some seriously hefty wrecking bars out there but, again, we're limited on space. That said, even a relatively small wrecking bar can prove useful for demolition purposes, prying apart boards, and removing stubborn nails.[13]

11. Bolt Cutters, 14"

Here, again, size matters. And a mere fourteen inches in length is small for bolt cutters. Truth be told, I should've tried to find eighteen-inch bolt cutters instead, as they would have still fit in my toolbox and have been easier to use as well.[14] Unfortunately, the truly useful bolt cutters of twenty-four or thirty-six inches in length are simply too long to fit in most any common toolbox. Nonetheless, even a small set of bolt cutters will eventually get the job done by "taking small bites" out of the job, if it comes to that.

More Cutting Tools

Here's a few more tools that make specific cutting tasks significantly easier...

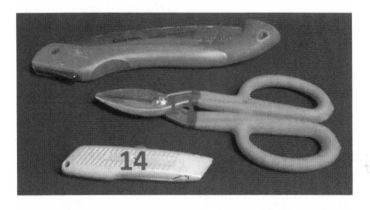

12. Folding Pruning Saw, 10"

While the small hand saw mentioned previously will certainly work for most every situation that this folding saw would be useful for, it never hurts to have more cutting tools, particularly one that's portable, easily wielded, and designed for cutting small tree branches. Such a tool could cut lumber if necessary, but their ultimate purpose is for gathering firewood.

13. Tin Snips

Think of tin snips as very heavy-duty scissors, capable of not only cutting thin sheet metal, but chicken wire, small nails or screws, and more.[15] Alternatively, a pair of aviation snips could prove just as useful, if not more so, than a pair of tin snips. In any case, tin snips or aviation snips are like much stronger scissors and may prove useful to you in the right situation.

Moreover, I'd suggest that a pair of bolt cutters would work even better in some instances than either tin snips or aviation snips if you can get the head of the bolt cutters in place, which isn't always easy considering how relatively bulky they are as compared to tin snips.

14. Utility Knife (with extra blades)

It's a small knife with disposable blades, what else needs said?

Hand Drill, Bit Set

You might not think that you'll ever need a hand drill or set of drill bits, especially when you could just nail most things together. That said, screws do hold better than nails over the long-term and can be used to draw pieces of wood together better than nails will, which makes these items potentially useful for some repair jobs.

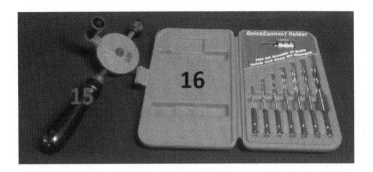

15. Manual Hand Drill

You may find that it's rather difficult to drive screws into wood that hasn't been pre-drilled. Oftentimes, using screws without pre-drilling holes can easily split wood and ruin that piece of wood. Thus, if the power is out, you're going to want to include a manual hand drill for this very reason.[16] They're not very fast and take some getting used to, but a hand drill will be indispensable for those times when nails just won't do.

16. Drill Bit Set

I thought about including a few dozen loose drill bits which I don't use instead of the small drill bit set shown here—and I may still do so—but I was thinking about including drill bit sizes which will work with the screws I included in this toolbox (shown later). With that in mind, this bit set is perfect for my purposes and protects the bits from being damaged or lost as well.

Pliers, Wrenches

A good set of pliers or a wrench set could be among the most important tools in your toolbox. Ensure you have both locking pliers (aka., vice-grips) and slip-joint pliers, which should cover most situations. Specialty wrenches, including the needle-nose and strap wrench, may be considered optional if you're tight on money or space in your toolbox.

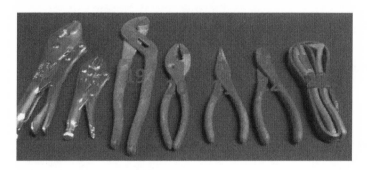

17. Locking Pliers, large

A good pair of locking pliers is essential in any toolbox, in my opinion.[17] Being able to grip and hold any number of items, from broken screwheads to stuck nuts, just makes things that much easier on you when it's already stressful enough.

18. Locking Pliers, small

Looking back, I probably should have included another large pair of locking pliers instead of a smaller set, but there could be times when the smaller set will fit in places that the larger set won't. For that reason, and that reason alone, I've included a small set of locking pliers as well.

19. Slip-Joint Pliers, large

I can't tell you how many times I've used a pair of large slip-joint pliers, from common household repairs to bending things I probably shouldn't be bending, they're invaluable and very easy to use.

20. Slip-Joint Pliers, small

Pliers are like hammers in so much as there are a wide variety of styles. Most styles aren't useful for our purposes, though, another, small set sometimes proves useful to have.

21. Needle-Nose Pliers

Sometimes only a pair of needle-nose pliers will fit where you need them to; have a pair in your toolbox for precisely those instances.

22. Wire Cutters

Wire cutters may be useful in very limited situations and, in my opinion, aren't very necessary to include, but they came with the set and I'd hate to "break up the band," so to speak.

23. Strap Wrench, small

When I'm around plumbing, it seems that a strap wrench is the only tool I have on hand which will work for the job. And, while there are different sizes of strap wrenches, even a small one (like the one shown) should work for most any around-the-house repair that I can think of. If you're unsure of what you may need then include a set of varying sizes to cover your bases.[18]

Ratchet and Sockets

Just as with pliers, a good socket set may be just the thing you need...

24. Socket Set (with 1/4-inch drive ratchet)

I was going to include a set of wrenches in my toolbox but figured that the slips wrenches would be adequate stand-ins; for all other times a ratchet and socket would be preferred. Ensure the socket set covers a wide range of sizes (in both standard and metric) and includes an extension.[19] Though not ideal, this socket set includes a 1/4-inch drive ratchet that will get most small jobs done. If you know you have need for a heavier-duty 3/8-inch or 1/2-drive ratchet, then include one too.

25. 1/4-inch Drive Ratchet (alternative to socket set)

Alternatively, you could simply include a single ratchet and a universal socket (discussed next) if you're short on space in your toolbox.

26. Universal Socket (alternative to socket set)

As the name suggests, this universal socket can replace a range of sockets.[20] My experience with them is that they're never ideal and only occasionally truly useful. I went ahead and included one in my toolbox because it was so small. If you really need to save space in your toolbox, then it will work for most jobs… just not very well.

Cordage, Zip Ties, Velcro

Cordage may be less useful than most of the tools already mentioned thus far. That said, cordage can make some tasks easier, such as with strapping down a load in your truck, securing tools, lashing, replacing broken straps, and more.

Looking back, I should've just added more of the paracord and not have included the bungee cords. The zip ties and Velcro may or may not be useful.

27. Zip/Wire Ties, dozens (15" or similar length)

Zip ties always seem to be useful for some reason or another, yet I never seem to have enough on hand. And, while there are a wide range of lengths, you may as well include longer zip ties (I choose fifteen-inch ties) as they'll likely be more useful overall and can be trimmed, if needed.

28. Bungee Cords, several (of different sizes)

I choose to include a handful of bungee cords of varying lengths as well. These cords aren't very good, that's for sure, but they'll probably do what I need them to. Like I said, I may eventually replace them with more paracord.

29. 550 Paracord (25+ feet)

For those times where the bungee cords won't work, paracord should. Really, most any cordage may prove useful, from twine to actual rope, but considering how strong paracord is relatively to size and weight, it was a no-brainer to include some. I included about twenty-five feet but should've included more; I'd say 50-75 feet should be enough for scenarios that I can imagine.

30. Velcro Strap (optional)

This Velcro strap is self-adhering and can be reused repeatedly. Truth be told, there aren't too many scenarios where I can imagine this Velcro strap being used. As such, it's optional to include in your toolbox.

Staple Gun

Although small nails may work in place of staples for a short period of time, a staple gun makes tacking down items like plastic sheeting or tarps fast and easy. In addition, staples are often more secure than nails when used to secure plastic sheeting, for instance, because nails may quickly rip through the plastic when the wind picks up.

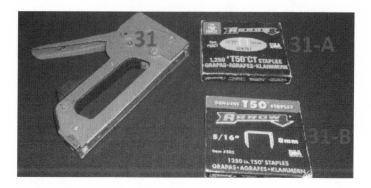

31. Staple Gun (with various staples sizes)

This staple gun I included in this toolkit is an old gun. There are newer, heavy-duty guns which are surely better.[21] Regardless, be sure to include plenty of staples; a few hundred should be plenty. I choose to include two different sizes, but if I had to pick just one then something around the 3/8" or 10 mm length should be generally useful.

Clamps

I've found that quick-release clamps are about the best thing since sliced bread, maybe you have as well. They're very easy to adjust, hold tight, and are superior to most any other clamp I've ever used. That said, a pair of hand spring clamps work well in certain situations and are relatively small; there's no harm in adding a few of these too. Here's the quick-release clamps that I use:

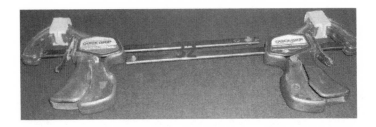

32. Quick-Release Clamps

While there are plenty of different sizes I choose a set of clamps that's twelve inches in length which should be long enough for most purposes, yet still fit in my toolbox.[22] You may find that a longer set would be even better. Be sure to include at least two clamps.

Screwdrivers, Bit Set, Allen Wrench Set, Star Key Set

The important part here is to have a relatively wide variety of bits to rely upon, hence, the inclusion of the bit set, item #34. After thinking about this some more, I really should purchase another, bigger Allen wrench set because the one I included here doesn't have larger sizes that I may need.

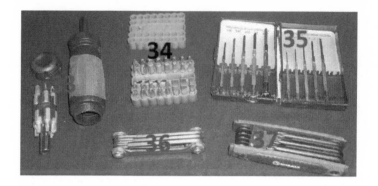

33. Multi-Bit Screwdriver

If you have the room then consider including a full set of Philips- and flat-head screwdrivers, or you could just toss in a multi-bit screwdriver like I did.[23] Originally, I was trying to save weight and conserve space, but that idea went out of the window a long time ago, lol.

34. Screwdriver Bit Set

A quality bit set extends the use of my multi-bit screwdriver immensely. Just be sure the bit set includes a variety of different bits not included with the multi-bit screwdriver and that they fit into the end of multi-bit screwdriver because sometimes they don't.

35. Precision Screwdriver Set (optional)

Commonly known as "eyeglass screwdrivers," this set is only useful for small electronic repairs. With that in mind, this set is optional. That said, if you ever actually need a very small screwdriver and don't have it, well... don't say I didn't tell you to add them.

36. Allen Wrench Set

Occasionally, an Allen wrench will be necessary. And, while there are many different sizes you could include, a basic set like this one should cover most instances. If you really want to be thorough, you could include both a metric and standard Allen wrench set, but they're usually close enough in size that you can make one fit the other with a little luck and ingenuity.

37. Star Key Set

I can't even tell you the last time I had to use a star key for anything. As such, I wouldn't worry too much about including a set.

Assorted Tools

Here's where things begin to get haphazard as I simply photographed many of the smaller items together...

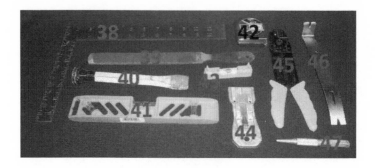

38. Carpenter's Framing Square, 12" x 6"

Although you can makeshift a square with a book cover or any number of items, for that matter, just save yourself the trouble and get a small framing square and be done with it. An even better option would be a triangular speed square.[24]

39. Metal File (for sharpening blade edges)

Occasionally I'll sit sharpen my tools or wood-splitting axe. It's a bit of work, no doubt, but well-worth the time and effort because a well-honed edge makes the job that much easier and even extends their longevity. Get yourself a quality metal file because the odds are that you'll need to sharpen something sooner or later after a disaster.

For knives (or anything with a very sharp edge, such as the utility knife) you're going to want a ceramic whetstone or sharpening stone—preferably one that's double-sided—though, even a mini whetstone will get the job done.

40. Cold Chisel

I can't even remember what I used this for last, but I do know that if I didn't have it in my toolbox yet needed a cold chisel then I would be kicking myself for not including one. With that in mind, a cold chisel can be useful for removing old bolts or nuts, splitting bricks and apparently for working sheet metal, which I don't do. You may as well just get a set of them.[25]

41. Torpedo Level

About the only reason I ever use a level is to hang my wife's many pictures, lol. I included one here because I had an extra and I'm sure there's some construction purpose where a level is useful to someone.

42. Tape Measure, 25' or longer

Originally (at least, in the photo) I included a twelve-foot tape measure to save weight, but later swapped it out with a longer, twenty-five-foot tape measure which could prove more useful.

43. Mini Level (optional)

This is optional as the torpedo level will do everything this level can.

44. Razor Blade Scraper (with extra blades, not shown)

A razor blade scraper is mostly meant to clean or prepare surfaces, such as by removing old caulking or adhesive, and may be used in place of a utility knife. Be sure to include additional blades too.

45. Wire Strippers

This set of wire strippers is nothing to get excited about and can probably be replaced by the wire cutters and pliers mentioned previously. Nevertheless, a pair of wire strippers does work better for their intended purpose than the aforementioned suggestions, especially for stripping the ends of wiring and properly crimping electrical wire "crimp" caps.

46. Mini Utility Bar, 7"

There are a few spaces when my claw hammer just won't fit properly to remove a stubborn nail; this mini utility par usually gets the job done.

47. Nail Punch (optional)

This is another one of those small and lightweight, yet probably not necessary items to include. Regardless, a nail punch (aka. "center punch") can be used to drive finishing nails without damaging wood as well as for "centering" the hole so that a drill bit doesn't "wander."

Caulk Gun

Sometimes you may need to ensure a repair job never comes apart. If so, construction adhesive is just the thing you want. Other times you may need to use caulking to properly seal out water. In either case, a caulking gun is necessary.

48. Caulk Gun (with heavy-duty adhesive)

Caulking is meant to seal out water and wind intrusion whereas a construction adhesive—especially heavy-duty exterior liquid nails like I have pictured above—is great to also have because it holds well and seals almost everything, from wood and drywall to plastic and concrete. Consider including two tubes to ensure you have enough for a big repair job.

And, although I didn't include any in mine, a can of foam insulation would be good to have as well for those times when you need to seal a hole or two quickly or for when you have an awkward repair job that the foam would be better suited to fix than adhesive.

Siphon Hose

These are great for quickly transferring liquid, especially gasoline...

49. Gas Siphon (shaker hose)

I've become accustomed to using a "shaker hose" to quickly and easily transfer gasoline from my five-gallon gas cans to my vehicles when it's time to swap out stored gas. These hoses make it VERY easy and much faster to do so, and with less mess too.

No doubt that a siphon hose can certainly be used to transfer any liquid, even water.[26] Just remember that if this hose is ever used for anything harmful to you (such as gasoline) that it cannot EVER be used for a potable substance afterwards, no matter how well you think you cleaned it. Therefore, be sure to mark the siphon hose properly and prominently if it's ever been used for anything you cannot directly consume.

Security Cable, Lock

A security cable may or may not find use for you after disaster. Add one only if you think you'll have a need.

50. Heavy-Duty Security Cable

Who knows what you may need to secure, from your generator to a gate, including a heavy-duty security cable never hurts.[27] And because it's quite a bit stronger than a common bicycle locking cable, it's usually a better choice.

51. Keyed Lock (to go with security cable)

You're going to need a quality lock as well. I prefer a keyed lock for this purpose, but even a combination lock will work and may be preferable if you're prone to losing keys.

Extension Cable

Here, again, is another optional item to include...

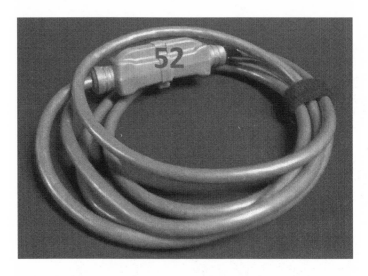

52. Electrical Extension Cord (optional)

I choose to include a several-foot extension cord even though I'm not planning on grid power being available. Why? It's one of those "you never know" items coupled with the fact that I had space available in my toolbox.

Miscellaneous

We're finally down to a variety of items that may be small yet could prove invaluable, especially the duct tape and flashlight...

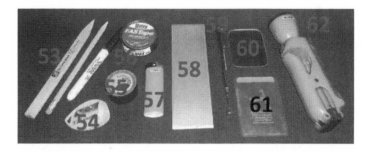

53. Pencils and Markers

I like to include a variety of marking supplies, specifically pencils and permanent markers; if I had to choose, however, go with a pencil or two since they'll never dry out and can mark almost anything.

54. Pencil Sharpener

No doubt that the utility knife will get the job done to make a pencil useful again, but a pencil sharpener gets the job done better, easier, and with the least amount of pencil shavings lost.

55. Electrical Tape

In most cases, duct tape will probably work fine, but electrical tape is designed to NOT be conductive and is also less likely to become brittle or breakdown over longer periods of time. If you expect to have to repair electrical wiring at all then include a roll of electrical tape to cover yourself properly.

56. Plumbers Teflon Tape

Like electrical tape, only Teflon tape will truly seal plumbing threads properly. You may be tempted to include plumber's putty instead (which could be a useful addition for some repairs), but putty will dry out over time whereas tape is always ready to be used.

57. Bic Lighter

Besides just having the ability to start a fire, you could need a lighter to ignite a butane or propane torch, melt cordage ends, or warm up a bottle of glue. And did I mention they start fires? That's always a great reason to have a lighter around.

58. Duct Tape, roll

Here, again, I tried to save space by wrapping several feet of duct tape around a piece of cardboard. Later, I figured that saving a few ounces wasn't necessary and choose to include an entire roll of duct tape (not shown in the photo above). Considering just how useful duct tape can be, that was a wise decision, and I encourage you to do the same.

59. Magnetic Telescoping Pick Up Tool

Dropping that last bolt, nut, or screw into a hard-to-reach place can make finishing an otherwise easy repair job very frustrating. A magnetic telescoping tool, such as this one, can be a life-saver. I know, I've been there a few times.

60. Mirror, small

Similarly, just being able to see the backside of an object can make a repair easier too, and a handy mirror like this one can save the day! Know, too, that you can get telescoping mirrors if that interests you.

61. Magnifying Glass

The older I get the harder it is to read fine print or small markings on supplies. I choose to include a credit-card-style Fresnel lens magnifying glass— which is about 3x magnification—but if you can get an actual magnifier that's, say, 10x magnification or better then go for it.

62. Flashlight (with extra batteries)

You've got to include a flashlight in your toolkit, especially if it conveniently clamps to a workbench like this one does. Even a headlamp is a great choice because it leaves both hands free to use. No matter which light you choose, include extra batteries and, if possible, do NOT leave batteries installed in the flashlight in the event they leak and corrode the terminals.

Supplies

Lubricants have so many potential uses, though, there's no guarantee that you'll need any for home repair purposes after a disaster. The epoxy, on the other hand, is great to include because it can bond so many different items.

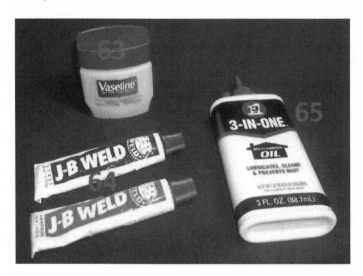

63. Petroleum Jelly, small jar

A small jar of Vaseline can be useful for a variety of reasons, including as a lubricant for locks, repelling rust on tools, combating corrosion on battery terminals, and even as a fire-starting aid.

64. J-B Weld (and/or strong glue)

A two-part epoxy, J-B Weld bonds almost anything, and can be used to permanently bond a variety of substances, including metal, concrete, PVC, glass and more. It's great for a variety of household repairs, auto and marine repairs, as well as some plumbing jobs.

Alternatively, you could opt for a strong glue, such as Gorilla Glue (my current favorite), instead of an epoxy like this. Surely there's no harm in having both; I should include a bottle of glue myself.

65. 3-in-1 Household Oil

Use it to lubricate moving parts or protect tools and gear from rust—much like Vaseline does—a little goes a long way, especially for most any household use that I can think of.

Sundries

Include plenty of nails and screws of varying lengths as well as some other items we'll discuss shortly...

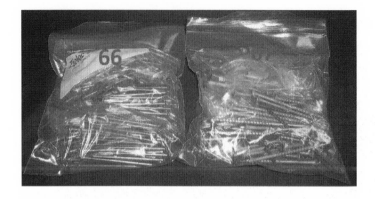

66. Nails (of varying sizes)

Include an assortment of nails, from smaller finishing nails to longer deck nails. Whatever you can include here is great. Personally, I've included dozens of about three or four different sizes myself which should be enough for most any repair that I can do myself.

67. Other Sundries (screws, nuts and bolts, wire caps, etc.)

Similarly, I choose to include a variety of screws, as well as an assortment of nuts and bolts, washers, hex-head screws, and electrical wire caps (both crimp-on and screw-on). Any small sundries that you may think of are great to include here as well if you have the space.

Getting Everything Inside My Toolbox

As you can see below, I was able to fit all the tools and supplies inside with a bit of room to spare:

I wonder what else I can fit in there? If you have any suggestions, do let me know.

We're almost done, read on to see where else you might add a few hand tools...

Bonus #1: Vehicle Tools

I've also been thinking about tools for very basic vehicle repairs and/or tools that may prove useful during a bug out. Besides the items that everyone should keep in their car in the event of a vehicle breakdown—specifically a set of jumper cables and items to repair a flat tire, such as a tire repair kit and 12-volt air compressor or even a bicycle hand pump—there's no harm in also including a few additional hand tools:

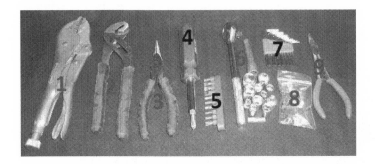

1. Locking Pliers
2. Slip-Joint Pliers
3. Needle-Nose Pliers
4. Multi-Bit Screwdriver
5. Screwdriver Bit Set
6. Ratchet and Socket Set (with extension)
7. Allen Wrench Set
8. Blade Fuses (assorted, and appropriate to my car)
9. Longer Needle-Nose Pliers (specifically for replacing fuses)

FYI: You don't see a hammer included in the tools pictured above because I decided to include this survival axe that I reviewed in my set of tools which also functions as a hammer.[28]

I would also strongly encourage you to include an entire roll of duct tape (not shown) because it can be used for a variety of oddball vehicles repairs, such as to seal a radiator hose, cover broken glass, hold body panels together, and more. Be sure to include a heavy-duty brand or "industrial" strength tape rather than the basic strength tape because it's less likely to tear and, more importantly, is much stickier and more likely to stay put.

Of course, if you have the space to spare in your vehicle as well as the time to grab this entire survival toolbox during a bug out situation then do that because there are many more items that may prove useful to you.

Bonus #2: Everyday Carry Tool

I couldn't end this discussion on hand tools without a brief mention of what you might keep on your person, also known as everyday carry or "EDC" for short. Once upon a time, I used to keep a lot of gear on me, including my version of the ever-popular Altoid's survival kits, things attached to my keychain, supplies in my wallet, and more. It started to get out of hand, to say the least.[29, 30]

I still keep most items on my keychain and in my wallet, but I'll also sometimes include this tool as well:

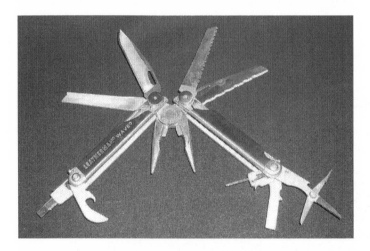

That's right, it's my handy Leatherman Wave multitool.[31] And it used to be that I wouldn't leave home without it but, sadly, I get lazy too and tend not to have it with me when I leave the house anymore, especially when it's summertime.

That's my bad. It's a good tool and quite useful, since it includes pliers, a knife, a mini saw that isn't too shabby, as well as various other tools that may or may not be of use. Personally, I've used them all at one point or another, but it's really the main three which I've mentioned already that are potentially the most useful to your survival, in my opinion.

There are, no doubt, many other options available. Whatever you choose, a multitool is always a good addition and will be there for you so long as you choose to include one in your daily EDC gear.

Concluding Thoughts

If you have any experience with common household repairs, then most everything discussed herein shouldn't be a surprise. After all, they're typical hand tools that serve a specific purpose. Every item was included because it does a job and does it very well. Remember that there's nothing like NOT having a hammer when you need one. The same can be said for a saw, pair of pliers, or screwdriver, to name a few tools that you should never be without after a disaster.

You should also realize that this toolkit isn't solely for maintaining and repairing your home after a disaster, as it could prove useful for repairing your vehicles (to a small degree) and even important survival equipment, such as a generator.

Now, if you had to start with only a handful of items due to expense then go with the very basics: hammer, hand saw and hacksaw, slip-joint pliers, screwdriver and bit set, and maybe the tape measure. The wrecking bar, tin snips, staple gun, and clamps would probably be next on my list, followed closely by the sundries (nails, screws, etc.), duct tape, and exterior adhesive.

Don't forget the safety gear either, especially safety glasses, ear plugs, and gloves. Understand, too, that it's likely just as important to have a hard hat in your prepping supplies as any other safety gear even though it won't fit in a toolbox because of the potential for falling debris after a disaster.

All additional tools and supplies can be added at your convenience. Like I said before, there's no rush. Take your time and look at local garage sales or thrift stores and ask friends or family if they have extra tools you might have. With a little effort you'll have a quality survival toolbox gathered in no time.

Finally, remember to NOT keep this toolbox anywhere near your main gathering of tools in case they become compromised, such as by a falling tree. Instead, keep the toolbox well away, even in the trunk of your car, if you must.

And, while you're at it, put together a small set of hand tools for your vehicles so have something to rely upon during a bug out and, if you're so inclined, add a quality multitool to your EDC gear; I prefer the Leatherman Wave, but there are plenty of other options to choose from.

Get Your Free Checklist Here

Before you grab your checklist, be a good friend or family member and choose to help others who could use this crucial information...

Spread the Word, Share the Knowledge

I'm willing to bet that you have family and friends who could benefit from this book as well, so please take a moment right now and quickly share a link to it on Facebook, Twitter, or Pinterest... you can easily do so here.[32]

Now, download your free, easy-to-reference 67-point toolbox checklist here.[33]

Discover More Survival Books Here

If you liked what you read within then you're going to love my other survival books.[34] Here's a sampling:

- 53 Essential Bug Out Bag Supplies[35]
- 47 Easy DIY Survival Projects[36]
- The Complete Pet Safety Action Plan[37]
- 28 Powerful Home Security Solutions[38]
- 27 Crucial Smartphone Apps for Survival[39]
- 57 Scientifically-Proven Survival Foods to Stockpile[40]
- 75 of the Best Secret Hiding Places[41]
- Your Identity Theft Protection Game Plan[42]
- 144 Survival Uses for 10 Common Items[43]
- 9.0 Cascadia Earthquake Survival[44]

And if you would like to be among the first to know when new survival books become available, fill out this form and you'll be notified via email.[45]

Recommended for You...

I want to point out one book from the above list, in particular, since you clearly recognize the need to prepare for emergencies: *47 Easy DIY Survival Projects: How to Quickly Get Your Family Prepared for Emergencies in Only 10 Minutes a Day*.

Here's a small portion of what's covered inside, including:

- How to store water easily, properly treat it when needed, and quickly stockpile more;
- How to create an emergency binder, document possessions quickly, and prepare your pets;
- How to make homemade MREs, boost vitamin yields of grains, and start container gardening;
- How to use a thermos to cook, build a 30-second rocket stove and vegetable can stove;
- How to make homemade cleaners, rodent traps, makeshift lamps, and a DIY Faraday cage;
- How to get your bedside ready for emergencies, create a bug out bag, and pocket survival kit;
- How to develop personal disaster response plans, earthquake-proof shelving, and always get alerts.

Discover how to quickly get your family prepared for emergencies in only ten minutes a day with these 47 easy DIY survival projects.[46]

Your Opinion Matters to Me

I'd love to hear your feedback about this book, especially anything I might be able to add or improve upon for future revisions. Please send me an email at rethinksurvival@gmail.com with the word "book" in the subject if you have something for me. (And be sure to include the book title so I'm not confused.)

Why You Should Review This Book...

Because reviews are critical in spreading the word about books, I ask that you take a moment and write a review of the book so that others know what to expect, particularly if you've found my advice useful.[47]

I do hope that you've enjoyed this book and that you will choose to add my recommendations to your survival toolbox to help you and your family stay safe from disasters of all kinds, big or small.

I encourage you to please take a moment and download the checklist above, share this book with your friends and family using the link I provided previously, and leave a quick review on Amazon.com while you're at it.

May God bless you and your family. Thank you for your time, Damian

Appendices

Appendix A: 67-Point Checklist

Appendix B: List of Resources

Appendix A: 67-Point Checklist

Safety Gear

1. Dust Masks, several (preferably N-95 rated)

2. Safety Glasses

3. Ear Protection (e.g., ear plugs)

4. Leather Gloves, fitted

5. Larger Work Gloves (bonus if fitted gloves can also fit inside)

6. Chemical Gloves, heavy-duty preferred

Cutting Tools

7. Crosscut Hand Saw, 15"

8. Hacksaw (with extra blades)

Hammer, Wrecking Bar, Bolt Cutter

9. Claw Hammer, 16 oz.

10. Wrecking Bar, 18"

11. Bolt Cutters, 14"

More Cutting Tools

12. Folding Pruning Saw, 10"

13. Tin Snips / Aviation Snips

14. Utility Knife (with extra blades)

Hand Drill, Bit Set

15. Manual Hand Drill

16. Drill Bit Set

Pliers, Wrenches

17. Locking Pliers, large

18. Locking Pliers, small

19. Slip-Joint Pliers, large

20. Slip-Joint Pliers, small

21. Needle-Nose Pliers

22. Wire Cutters

23. Strap Wrench, small

Ratchet and Sockets

24. Socket Set (with ¼-inch drive ratchet)

25. 1/4" Drive Ratchet (alternative to socket set)

26. Universal Socket (alternative to socket set)

Cordage, Zip Ties, Velcro

27. Zip/Wire Ties, dozens (15" or similar length)

28. Bungee Cords, several (of different sizes)

29. 550 Paracord (25+ feet)

30. Velcro Strap (optional)

Staple Gun

31. Staple Gun (with various staples sizes)

Clamps

32. Quick-Release Clamps and/or spring clamps

Screwdrivers, Bit Set, Etc.

33. Multi-Bit Screwdriver

34. Screwdriver Bit Set

35. Precision Screwdriver Set (optional)

36. Allen Wrench Set

37. Star Key Set

Assorted Tools

38. Carpenter's Framing Square, 12" x 6"

39. Metal File (for sharpening blade edges)

40. Cold Chisel

41. Torpedo Level

42. Tape Measure, 25' or longer

43. Mini Level (optional)

44. Razor Blade Scraper (with extra blades)

45. Wire Strippers

46. Mini Utility Bar, 7"

47. Nail Punch (optional)

Caulk Gun

48. Caulk Gun (with heavy-duty adhesive)

Siphon Hose

49. Gas Siphon (shaker hose)

Security Cable, Lock

50. Heavy-Duty Security Cable

51. Keyed Lock (to go with security cable)

Extension Cable

52. Electrical Extension Cord (optional)

Miscellaneous

53. Pencils and Markers

54. Pencil Sharpener

55. Electrical Tape

56. Plumbers Teflon Tape

57. Bic Lighter

58. Duct Tape, roll

59. Magnetic Telescoping Pick Up Tool

60. Mirror, small

61. Magnifying Glass

62. Flashlight (with extra batteries)

Supplies

63. Petroleum Jelly, small jar

64. J-B Weld (and/or strong glue)

65. 3-in-1 Household Oil

Sundries

66. Nails (of varying sizes)

67. Other Sundries (screws, nuts and bolts, etc.)

Appendix B: List of Resources

- Link 1: https://rethinksurvival.com/books/survival-toolbox-checklist.php
- Link 2: https://rethinksurvival.com/books/survival-toolbox-book-offer.php
- Link 3: https://rethinksurvival.com/kindle-books/
- Link 4: https://rethinksurvival.com/kindle-books/survival-toolbox-recommends/#mask
- Link 5: https://www.todayshomeowner.com/how-to-choose-a-respirator-or-dust-mask/
- Link 6: https://rethinksurvival.com/kindle-books/survival-toolbox-recommends/#glasses
- Link 7: https://blog.safetyglassesusa.com/how-to-identify-ballistic-rated-eyewear/
- Link 8: https://www.coopersafety.com/earplugs-noise-reduction
- Link 9: https://ehs.berkeley.edu/workplace-safety/glove-selection-guide
- Link 10: https://rethinksurvival.com/kindle-books/survival-toolbox-recommends/#gloves

- Link 11: https://rethinksurvival.com/kindle-books/survival-toolbox-recommends/#saw
- Link 12: https://www.youtube.com/watch?v=sTRpL mZqS6w
- Link 13: https://rethinksurvival.com/kindle-books/survival-toolbox-recommends/#bar
- Link 14: https://rethinksurvival.com/kindle-books/survival-toolbox-recommends/#bolt
- Link 15: https://rethinksurvival.com/kindle-books/survival-toolbox-recommends/#snips
- Link 16: https://rethinksurvival.com/kindle-books/survival-toolbox-recommends/#drill
- Link 17: https://rethinksurvival.com/kindle-books/survival-toolbox-recommends/#pliers
- Link 18: https://rethinksurvival.com/kindle-books/survival-toolbox-recommends/#strap
- Link 19: https://rethinksurvival.com/kindle-books/survival-toolbox-recommends/#socket
- Link 20: https://rethinksurvival.com/kindle-books/survival-toolbox-recommends/#universal
- Link 21: https://rethinksurvival.com/kindle-books/survival-toolbox-recommends/#staplegun
- Link 22: https://rethinksurvival.com/kindle-books/survival-toolbox-recommends/#clamps

The Survival Toolbox

- Link 23: https://rethinksurvival.com/kindle-books/survival-toolbox-recommends/#screwdriver
- Link 24: https://rethinksurvival.com/kindle-books/survival-toolbox-recommends/#square
- Link 25: https://rethinksurvival.com/kindle-books/survival-toolbox-recommends/#chisel
- Link 26: https://rethinksurvival.com/kindle-books/survival-toolbox-recommends/#siphon
- Link 27: https://rethinksurvival.com/kindle-books/survival-toolbox-recommends/#cable
- Link 28: https://rethinksurvival.com/off-grid-tools-survival-axe-review/
- Link 29: https://rethinksurvival.com/so-youve-got-your-edc-covered-but-what-about-your-spouse/
- Link 30: https://rethinksurvival.com/whats-in-your-wallet-heres-14-items-in-mine-and-what-probably-should-be-in-yours/
- Link 31: https://rethinksurvival.com/kindle-books/survival-toolbox-recommends/#leatherman
- Link 32: https://rethinksurvival.com/books/survival-toolbox-share.html
- Link 33: https://rethinksurvival.com/books/survival-toolbox-checklist.php

70

- Link 34: https://rethinksurvival.com/kindle-books/
- Link 35: https://rethinksurvival.com/kindle-books/bug-out-bag-book/
- Link 36: https://rethinksurvival.com/kindle-books/diy-survival-projects-book/
- Link 37: https://rethinksurvival.com/kindle-books/pet-safety-plan-book/
- Link 38: https://rethinksurvival.com/kindle-books/home-security-book/
- Link 39: https://rethinksurvival.com/kindle-books/smartphone-survival-apps-book/
- Link 40: https://rethinksurvival.com/kindle-books/survival-foods-book/
- Link 41: https://rethinksurvival.com/kindle-books/secret-hides-book/
- Link 42: https://rethinksurvival.com/kindle-books/id-theft-book/
- Link 43: https://rethinksurvival.com/kindle-books/survival-uses-book/
- Link 44: https://rethinksurvival.com/kindle-books/earthquake-survival-book/
- Link 45: https://rethinksurvival.com/books/new-survival-books.php
- Link 46: https://rethinksurvival.com/kindle-books/diy-survival-projects-book/
- Link 47: https://rethinksurvival.com/books/survival-toolbox-review.php

Made in the USA
Columbia, SC
26 May 2020